THE FOUR HORSEMEN
OF THE
APOCALYPSE

THE FOUR HORSEMEN
OF THE
APOCALYPSE

MARK HITCHCOCK

Multnomah® Publishers *Sisters, Oregon*

THE FOUR HORSEMEN OF THE APOCALYPSE
published by Multnomah Publishers, Inc.

© 2004 by Mark Hitchcock
International Standard Book Number: 1-59052-333-4

Cover design by UDG DesignWorks, Inc.

Unless otherwise indicated, Scripture quotations are from:
New American Standard Bible® © 1960, 1977, 1995
by the Lockman Foundation. Used by permission.
Other Scripture quotations:
Holy Bible, New Living Translation (NLT)
© 1996. Used by permission of Tyndale House Publishers, Inc.
All rights reserved.

Multnomah is a trademark of Multnomah Publishers, Inc.,
and is registered in the U.S. Patent and Trademark Office.
The colophon is a trademark of Multnomah Publishers, Inc.

Printed in the United States of America

For information:
MULTNOMAH PUBLISHERS, INC.
POST OFFICE BOX 1720
SISTERS, OREGON 97759

Library of Congress Cataloging-in-Publication Data
Hitchcock, Mark.
    The Four Horsemen of the Apocalypse / Mark Hitchcock.
        p. cm. -- (End times answers ; #7)
    Includes bibliographical references.
        ISBN 1-59052-333-4
1. Four Horsemen of the Apocalypse. 2. End of the world. 3. Bible. N.T.
Revelation VI, 1-8--Criticism, interpretation, etc. I. Title. II. Series.
    BS2825.52.H58 2004
    228' .06--dc22   2004009995

04 05 06 07 08 09 10—10 9 8 7 6 5 4 3 2 1 0

To Steve Mortensen,
my lifelong friend and brother in Christ,
whose passion for the Lord and His truth
is unequaled.

CONTENTS

INTRODUCTION

In Revelation 6:1–8, the apostle John records what many consider the most vivid and powerful vision in all of Bible prophecy. This section of the book of Revelation is often referred to as the "Four Horsemen of the Apocalypse."

Just reading those five words sends a chill up my spine. And so does the full account in the pages of the last book of Scripture:

> Then I saw when the Lamb broke one of the seven seals, and I heard one of the four living creatures saying as with a voice of thunder, "Come." I looked, and behold, a white horse, and he who sat on it had a bow; and a crown was given to him, and he went out conquering and to conquer.
>
> When He broke the second seal, I heard the

second living creature saying, "Come." And another, a red horse, went out; and to him who sat on it, it was granted to take peace from the earth, and that men would slay one another; and a great sword was given to him.

When He broke the third seal, I heard the third living creature saying, "Come." I looked, and behold, a black horse; and he who sat on it had a pair of scales in his hand. And I heard something like a voice in the center of the four living creatures saying, "A quart of wheat for a denarius, and three quarts of barley for a denarius; and do not damage the oil and the wine."

When the Lamb broke the fourth seal, I heard the voice of the fourth living creature saying, "Come." I looked, and behold, an ashen horse; and he who sat on it had the name Death; and Hades was following with him. Authority was given to them over a fourth of the earth, to kill with sword and with famine and with pestilence and by the wild beasts of the earth.

This gripping imagery of four differently colored horses riding forth one by one across the world's landscape has captivated hearts and minds ever since the apostle John first received the vision on the island of Patmos in A.D. 95. In this vision, John sees four horses and their riders galloping across the earth, bringing deceit, destruction, and devastation.

More than twenty years ago, when I first began to study Bible prophecy in depth, I read Billy Graham's riveting book *Approaching Hoofbeats: The Four Horsemen of the Apocalypse.*

Many people may not realize that Dr. Graham has written several books on Bible prophecy. In fact, he may have written more books on end-time prophecy than on any other subject. Back in 1983, he penned these words in *Approaching Hoofbeats:*

> Some theologians and Bible scholars have thought these scenes as described by the apostle John to be a description of past events. However, most evangelical scholars interpret them as having to do with the future—as do I. In my view, the shadows of all four horsemen can already be seen galloping throughout the world at this

moment; therefore, I want not only to apply these four symbols of events yet to come, but also to put our ears to the ground and hear their hoofbeats growing louder by the day....

I can hear the hoofbeats of these horses much louder than when I first began writing this book....[1]

Over twenty years have passed since Billy Graham wrote those timely, sobering words. And if the hoofbeats of the four horsemen could be heard approaching in 1983, what about today, as we have passed into the new millennium? I believe we could safely say that the *approaching* hoofbeats have become *thundering* hoofbeats. Just think of all that's happened in the last two decades!

- The computer age has come, along with the Internet and unbelievable technology
- Militant Islam has risen as the world's most dangerous force
- Two Gulf Wars
- The eruption and continued escalation of violence in Israel

- The emergence and expansion of the European Union
- The 1990s "Decade of Globalization"
- 9/11
- The capture of Saddam Hussein

It's time to take another look at these four horsemen. It's time to step back for a moment and gain a fresh perspective on the events in our world today— events that so plainly foreshadow the fulfillment of John's apocalyptic vision.

- Who are these horsemen, and what do they mean for our world?
- Are there signs that they could be getting ready to mount up?
- Is there any hope for planet earth?
- Will man survive?

The four horsemen have always intrigued me. I've been drawn to these mysterious riders time and time again. It's always been one of my favorite prophetic portions in all of the Bible. I certainly don't profess to understand everything about them, but I have done my best to interpret their essential meaning and show how world events today seem to be ripe for their coming.

My prayer is that you will enjoy reading this book half as much as I enjoyed writing it. I believe if we listen carefully, putting an ear to the ground, we can hear the thunder of approaching hoofbeats.

A Quick, Aerial Overview

As with all the other books in my End Times Answers series, I make the assumption that the reader has at least a basic grasp of the main events of the end times. However, to help make sure that we're all on the same page, here's a brief overview of some of the key terms you will see sprinkled throughout this book.

The rapture of the church to heaven

The Rapture is an event that, from our human perspective, could occur at any moment. It's what we call a signless event. In other words, there is nothing left to be fulfilled before this event takes place. It is truly imminent. At the Rapture, all who have personally trusted Jesus Christ as their Savior, the living and the dead, will be caught up to meet the Lord in the air and will go with

Him back up to heaven. Then, at least seven years later, they will return again with Him, back to earth, at His Second Coming (John 14:1–3; 1 Corinthians 15:50–58; 1 Thessalonians 4:13–18).

The seven-year Tribulation period

The Tribulation is the final seven years of this age. It will begin with a peace treaty between Israel and Antichrist and will end with the second coming of Jesus Christ. During this time, the Lord will pour out His wrath upon earth in successive waves of judgment. But He will also pour out His grace, saving millions during these dark and terrible days (Revelation 6–19).

The three-and-a-half-year world empire of Antichrist

During the last half of the Tribulation, Antichrist will rule the world politically, economically, and religiously. The entire world will give allegiance to him— or suffer persecution and death (Revelation 13:1–18).

The campaign of Armageddon

The campaign or War of Armageddon is the final event of the Great Tribulation. It will occur when all the armies of the earth gather together to come against Israel and attempt once and for all to eradicate the Jewish people (Revelation 14:19–20; 16:12–16; 19:19–21).

The second coming of Christ to earth

The climactic event of human history is the literal, physical, visible, glorious return of Jesus Christ to planet earth. He will destroy the armies of the world, gathered in Israel, and will set up His kingdom on earth, which will last for a thousand years (Revelation 19:11–21).

God's Blueprint for the End Times

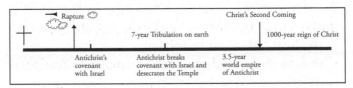

May the Lord use this book to help you hear the thunder of those four approaching riders—perhaps just over the horizon. And may He help all of us to be ready when Jesus comes to deliver His people from the wrath to come.

Maranatha!
Our Lord, Come!
Mark Hitchcock

RIDERS ON THE STORM

Horses and horsemen are mentioned some three hundred times in the Bible. But there aren't any that even come close to being as famous as the four horses—white, red, black, and pale—ridden by the four horsemen of the apocalypse.[2]

These four mysterious riders have always captivated the minds of men. We are drawn to them. There's something almost magnetic about their appeal.

They attract both believers and unbelievers alike. The scholar and the sensationalist. The passionate preacher and the merely curious.

Artists have been drawn to their imagery. I can't substantiate this with any hard data, but I believe that there are more artists' renditions of the four horsemen than of any other biblical image—except, perhaps, the Crucifixion and the Nativity. One of the most famous was painted by Albrecht Durer, a German artist of the Northern renaissance. In 1498, Durer created an artistic interpretation of the book of Revelation that included eighteen engravings of the Apocalypse. The most interesting of the engravings depicts the four horsemen. It's a stunning scene. The grim riders appear with dust clouds in their wake, trampling and destroying everything in their path.

Religious cults are also drawn to the four horsemen like bugs to a porch light. In his last days on earth, a young man named Vernon Wayne Howell, aka David Koresh, the self-proclaimed messiah, was poring over the four horsemen of the apocalypse in his Branch Davidian compound in Waco.

Together with over a hundred followers, Koresh held police and federal agents at bay outside his heavily armed compound. Koresh believed he was Jesus Christ, the Lamb of God, and the only one worthy and able to open the seven seals in Revelation 6 and bring about the end of the world. He believed that the events at his compound were the beginning of the end—and he was doing all he could to make this a self-fulfilling prophecy. The image of the four horsemen played over again and again in his warped mind.

Clearly, the four horsemen command people's attention. They should grab ours as well.

But as you get into this book you might be asking, "Why is this particular image so important? Why is it so vital for me to understand its message? Why have so many people focused attention on this vision down through the centuries?"

I would like to suggest four reasons.

HORSEPOWER

The first reason for the magnetism of the four horsemen is the powerful, vivid symbolism that's employed. Or, what we might call "horsepower."

In the Bible, horses often represent power, might, and awe. For the Jewish people, the horse was held in great awe and reverence. I have to be honest—I, too, hold horses in great awe. I've never had a positive experience riding horses the couple of times I've given it a try. I think they somehow sense my anxiety because they always decide to "take me for a ride." They have my utmost respect.

Job 39:19–25 contains a dramatic description of

the horse from the early days of man's history.

"Do you give the horse his might?
Do you clothe his neck with a mane?
Do you make him leap like the locust?
His majestic snorting is terrible.
He paws in the valley, and rejoices in his
    strength;
He goes out to meet the weapons.
He laughs at fear and is not dismayed;
And he does not turn back from the sword.
The quiver rattles against him,
The flashing spear and javelin.
With shaking and rage he races over the
    ground,
And he does not stand still at the voice of the
    trumpet.
As often as the trumpet sounds he says, 'Aha!'
And he scents the battle from afar,
And the thunder of the captains and the war
    cry."

Horses are awesome creatures. Nothing in the
world can compare with the sight and sound of a herd

of horses running at full throttle over the plains. Arguably, horses are the most beautiful creatures in the world. Nothing can touch their grandeur and majesty. Movies like *Seabiscuit* can move us to tears as we see the power, beauty, and drive of this regal animal.

Have you ever been to a racetrack and seen and heard the horses "coming down the stretch"? The rippling muscles. The flared nostrils. The thunderous sound. It's enthralling. Exhilarating.

The four horsemen are an awesome sight.

And a sight you never, never want to see.

THE NIGHT RIDERS OF ZECHARIAH

Second, horses represent more than just awe and respect in the Bible. Horses in the Bible frequently represent God's activity on earth and the forces He uses to accomplish His divine purposes. We see this clearly in the four horses mentioned in Zechariah 1:7–17 and 6:1–8.

In the earlier passage, the prophet sees a night rider on a red horse with red, brown, and white horses behind him. These four horses and riders are sent forth by God as a kind of horse patrol to "check things out" on the earth.

Again in Zechariah 6:1–8, the prophet sees four chariots, each drawn by different colored horses—red, black, white, and dappled. The four chariots come from between two bronze mountains. Bronze, in Scripture, often symbolizes judgment of sin. The four chariots are sent out to the north and the south to bring judgment on the nations who oppressed His people.

The imagery of the four horses in Revelation is undoubtedly connected to Zechariah's vision of different colored horses. From this obvious parallel, we know that the four horsemen in Revelation 6:1–8 are telling us something about God's coming judgment on the earth in the end times. This alone ought to grab our attention.

SILENT RIDERS

A third reason we are fascinated by these horsemen is their mystery. In each instance, when one of the angels cries *"erkou"* ("come"), a rider and horse gallop across the stage of history, summoned to thunder upon the earth. The imagery is striking, yet simple.

As the summons is issued to each horse and rider, one by one they hurtle across our world. And all it takes to describe these four riders is eight verses—two apiece. The brevity of each account leaves us wanting more. And most mysterious of all, none of the horsemen says a single word. They are mute. Each rides forth in complete silence. In another sense, however, they speak loudly to a world in desperate need of answers.

SCENE ONE OF THE END TIMES

Fourth, the four horsemen are important and captivating because they introduce the dreaded seven-year Tribulation. They represent scene one of the drama of the ages.

Revelation 6–19 is the fourteen-chapter heart of the book of Revelation. These chapters contain twenty-one judgments that will be unleashed on the world during the coming seven-year Tribulation period, leading up to the glorious appearing of Christ in Revelation 19. The twenty-one judgments are divided into three groups of seven.

Seven seals. Seven trumpets. Seven bowls.

The severity and scope of these judgments boggles the mind.

But before the seven trumpets and seven bowls are

SEVEN TRUMPET JUDGMENTS OF REVELATION 8–11	
First Trumpet (8:7)	Bloody Hail and Fire: One-Third of Vegetation Destroyed
Second Trumpet (8:8–9)	Fireball from Heaven: One-Third of Oceans Polluted
Third Trumpet (8:10–11)	Falling Star: One-Third of Fresh Water Polluted
Fourth Trumpet (8:12)	Darkness: One-Third of Sun, Moon, and Stars Darkened
Fifth Trumpet (9:1–12)	Demonic Invasion: Torment
Sixth Trumpet (9:13–21)	Demonic Army: One-Third of Mankind Killed
Seventh Trumpet (11:15–19)	The Kingdom: The Announcement of Christ's Reign

poured out on the earth, there are seven seal judgments. And the first of these four seal judgments is the four horses and riders in Revelation 6:1–8. So as you can see, the four horsemen will get it all started. The real action of Revelation, of the seven-year Tribulation, is introduced with these four horsemen. Through these symbols, God depicts the unleashing of the first four great judgments of the Tribulation period.

SEVEN BOWL JUDGMENTS OF REVELATION 16	
First Bowl (v. 2)	Upon the earth: Sores on the Worshipers of the Antichrist
Second Bowl (v. 3)	Upon the Seas: Turned to Blood
Third Bowl (vv. 4–7)	Upon the Fresh Water: Turned to Blood
Fourth Bowl (vv. 8–9)	Upon the Sun: Intense, Scorching Heat
Fifth Bowl (vv. 10–11)	Upon the Antichrist's Kingdom: Darkness and Pain
Sixth Bowl (vv. 12–16)	Upon the River Euphrates: Armageddon
Seventh Bowl (vv. 17–21)	Upon the Air: Earthquakes and Hail

For this reason, if we want to know what could be right around the corner for our planet, Revelation 6:1–8 is the place to begin. There's no more relevant passage for today in all of Bible prophecy.

THE CALM BEFORE THE STORM

I'm excited, as I hope you are, to jump right in and identify these four horsemen. But before we look at each individually, we need (as always) to gain a basic understanding of the setting and context for this great prophecy. And the introduction to the four horsemen is found in the heavenly scene in Revelation 4–5.

Ironically, it will take a quick trip to heaven to show us what on earth is going to happen in the future.

BEFORE THE STAMPEDE

I have always been fascinated by books and movies about time machines. There's something magical and mysterious about someone going back in time or catapulting into some future era. Movies like the *Back to the Future* trilogy or *Time After Time* never fail to grab me.

The book of Revelation could be viewed as a kind of biblical time machine. Revelation 1 records the description of the glorified Christ that John saw in A.D. 95 while exiled on the island of Patmos.

Revelation 2–3 records Christ's messages to the seven churches—solemn, powerful words that apply to all churches during this current church age. But Revelation 4–22 jets us forward into a time that's still future even in our day—the final days of planet earth as we know it.

Revelation 4:1–2 says:

> After these things I looked, and behold, a door standing open in heaven, and the first voice which I had heard, like the sound of a trumpet speaking with me, said, "Come up here, and I will show you what must take place after these things." Immediately I was in the Spirit; and behold, a throne was standing in heaven, and One sitting on the throne.

John is "in the Spirit," which means he was spiritually relocated. In this context, the phrase carries the idea that John's spirit was brought into direct contact with the invisible spiritual world—yet in ways that could still accommodate his finite human abilities and perception. In this trancelike state, John received revelation concerning things that will take place "after these things." That is, John received revelation about the future age. The age after the current church age, pictured in Revelation 2–3, has run its course.

We can see this three-fold division of Revelation reflected in Revelation 1:19, which serves as the basic outline of the entire book. This verse says, "Therefore write the things which you have seen, and the things which are, and the things which shall take place after these things."

- **Revelation 1** contains the things John has just seen (the glorified Christ).
- **Revelation 2–3** contain the things that are (the present church age).
- **Revelation 4–22** contain "the things that will occur after these things" (notice the presence of the same phrase "after these things" in Revelation 1:19 and 4:1).

In Revelation 4, the elderly apostle John is transported from the island of Patmos in A.D. 95—in a kind of spiritual time machine—to the final few years of this age, beyond where you and I are living now. John is "in the Spirit."

Before John receives the vision of the four horsemen on earth, however, he is transported to heaven to get a full view of God's throne and sovereignty. The backdrop for the four horsemen is the heavenly scene that introduces God as the Judge on His throne, a seven-sealed scroll in God's hand, and Jesus as the Lamb of God—the only one worthy to open the scroll and bring judgment. Since the four horsemen represent the first four of the seven seal judgments, let's look at the significance of this seven-sealed scroll.

THE SEVEN-SEALED SCROLL

Revelation 5:1 introduces us to a book, or more correctly a scroll, written on both sides and sealed up with seven seals. The fact that writing appears on both sides indicates the fullness of its contents. There is so much to be written that it "spills over" onto the back.[3]

The identity of this scroll has been debated down through the centuries. But in the context, the best interpretation seems to be that the scroll contains the revelation of God contained in the rest of the book of Revelation (6–22). For this reason, then, we could rightly call this the "scroll of doom," primarily focusing on the judgments of God leading to the establishment of Messiah's kingdom on the earth.

The seven seals on the scroll are there to keep its contents secret. Seals in that day were impressions made of clay, wax, or some other soft material that kept unauthorized persons from accessing the contents.[4] This only adds to the mystery. Each seal on the scroll must be broken one by one to divulge its contents.

As each seal is removed from the scroll, a little bit of the scroll is unrolled, each time revealing a worse horror. When the first seal is opened, John sees the first rider. The removal of the second seal allows a little more of the scroll to show, and the second horseman appears, and so on until the seventh seal is opened, which contains the seven trumpet judgments (Revelation 8:1–2). The judgments roll on until the entire scroll is opened, and Christ returns to establish His glorious kingdom on earth.

"On Earth As It Is in Heaven"

There is one other important structural feature of Revelation we need to understand: The scenes depicted in the book alternate between earth and heaven.

Revelation 4–5 offers a breathtaking view of heaven, centering around the very throne of God. The following two chapters, 6–7, focus on earthbound

Scene on earth	Revelation 1–3
Scene in heaven	Revelation 4–5
Scene on earth	Revelation 6–7
Scene in heaven	Revelation 8:1–5
Scene on earth	Revelation 8:6–14:20
Scene in heaven	Revelation 15
Scene on earth	Revelation 16:1–20:10
Scene in heaven	Revelation 20:11–22:21

events. Then, in 8:1–5, the scene switches back to heaven...and so it goes. What does this reveal to us? That the God who sits on the throne in heaven is in complete control of what transpires on earth. The events happening on earth—no matter how frightening and devastating—are neither haphazard nor random. They are ordered by the One seated on His throne. Heaven rules on earth.

As the songs of adoration and praise in heaven

cease, the Lamb of God begins to open the scroll. And this is a point we dare not miss. *Each of the four horsemen rides forth under the sovereign control and direction of Jesus Christ.* He releases them one by one as He breaks the seals on the scroll taken from the hand of God the Father. The horsemen are under the providential control of Christ, even though executed by human agency.

Revelation 6 shows that God is in total control of the future. All of the catastrophes that await our planet are part of the divine plan of the ages.

Jesus is the Sovereign Lamb who controls it all.

This is true of the great events of the past and future. And it's true of the events in your life and mine. This is a lesson none of us should ever forget!

HONING IN ON THE HORSEMEN

With this brief background in mind, we can now turn our attention to Revelation 6:1–8. Let these words of Billy Graham sink in, and prepare your heart as we move in for a closer look at the four horsemen.

> Imagine them as war-horses with heaving flanks and flared nostrils, rearing and pawing

the air with their terrible hooves. This kind of
horse stands out in both the biblical and historical narratives. It strikes fear in the heart of
the onlooker. The increasing sound of their
powerful hooves reverberates across our world
today. I ask you to join me as we explore what
the "four horsemen" are telling us—and God's
answer to the world's dilemma.[5]

CHAPTER THREE

THE RIDER ON THE WHITE HORSE

In Revelation 6:1, the scene changes dramatically. John is no longer in heaven. He is jolted back to earth with startling suddenness. No more throne in heaven. No more angels flying around the throne. No more twenty-four elders casting their crowns. No more heavenly choirs singing praises.

Talk about coming back to earth!

But God is not finished with John yet. In fact, his great vision of things to come is just beginning. God pulls back the corner of the veil on the future and allows John to peer into the final days of this age. At the breaking of the first seal, John gets his very first glimpse of the future time of worldwide tribulation.

And what he sees is a lone rider on a white charger, bent on conquest.

I saw when the Lamb broke one of the seven seals, and I heard one of the four living creatures saying as with a voice of thunder, "Come." I looked, and behold, a white horse, and he who sat on it had a bow; and a crown was given to him, and he went out conquering and to conquer. (Revelation 6:1–2)

FIRST THINGS FIRST

Who is this rider? And why a white horse?

Obviously, this is symbolic or figurative language. We don't expect a literal rider on a white horse to come riding out across the earth during the Tribulation. But we do expect that what this rider symbolizes will occur. Our job as students of the Bible, therefore, is to discover what this rider on the white horse really means.[6]

Four important textual factors in Revelation 6:1–2 must fit whatever view we adopt:

1. The white color of the horse
2. The bow in the rider's hand

3. The crown on the rider's head
4. The series of victories or conquests

There are four main views on the identity of the first horseman of the apocalypse. Let's look together at each of these and see which one best fits the language and context.

View #1:
The rider on the white horse is military conquest

Some believe this rider pictures the spirit of conquest or militarism, leading naturally to the bloodshed, poverty, and famine that follow in the next three horsemen. They point out that Revelation 6:2 says that the rider goes forth "conquering and to conquer."[7]

The main problem I have with this view is that the next horse, the red one, seems to clearly symbolize war and bloodshed. This would make the first two seals almost identical. What's more, the second seal, the rider on the red horse, takes peace from the earth (v. 4). For him to do so (obviously), peace must first exist. The conquest of that first rider, then, must represent the bloodless conquest of diplomacy and political subjugation.

View #2:
The rider on the white horse is the proclamation of the gospel

Commentator George Eldon Ladd writes:

> The rider is not Christ himself, but symbolizes the proclamation of the gospel of Christ in all the world. The details with which the first horseman is described do not weaken this conclusion. A bow is often used in Scripture as a symbol of divine victories.... This does not necessarily mean complete and utter conquest, but it does mean that the proclamation of the gospel will win its victories. It will be preached effectively in all the world; and in spite of an evil and hostile environment characterized by human hatred, strife, and opposition, the gospel will make its way victoriously in all the world.[8]

Ladd sees this as a great encouragement to the church in the face of stout opposition by the Roman empire.[9]

The chief problem with this view is that the four

horsemen are all to be taken together as a unit. And we must remember that they are all *judgments*. With this in mind, it would be strange for the preaching of the gospel to be included with the other horsemen, who leave nothing but destruction and devastation in their wake. What's more, in the parallel passage in Matthew 24:4–8, the judgments of the four horsemen are "the beginning of birth pains." To make the rider on the white horse the preaching of the gospel just seems out of place in this context.

View #3:
The rider on the white horse is Jesus Christ

One of the most popular views is that this rider represents Christ. Those who hold this position maintain that only Christ can ride a white horse. In the book of Revelation, the color white is consistently a symbol of Christ, or something associated with Him (1:14; 2:17; 3:4–5, 18; 4:4; 6:11; 7:9, 13; 14:14; 19:11, 14; 20:11).[10] For that matter, the rider on the white horse in Revelation 19:11–21 clearly *is* Christ, so why not view the rider on the white horse in Revelation 6 in the same light?

I believe that three compelling reasons explain

why the rider on the white horse *does not* represent Jesus.

First, there are clear contrasts between the riders in Revelation 6:2 and Revelation 19:11–19.

THE RIDER IN 6:2	THE RIDER IN 19:11–19
Carries a bow without any arrows	Wields a sword
Wears a *stephanos* or victor's crown	Wears many crowns—the *diadema* or kingly crown
Initiates war	Destroys His enemies and brings an end to war
Commences the Tribulation	Climaxes the Tribulation

This earlier rider bears the unmistakable marks of a counterfeit. The great preacher Donald Grey Barnhouse shows how diametrically opposed these two riders are:

We have only to look at the details of this prophecy to see how far removed this is from the Lord Jesus Christ of the Scriptures. The counterfeit is revealed by a detailed comparison of the two riders. The One whose name is the Word of God has on His head "many crowns." The symbol is of all royalty and majesty. The Greek word is diadem. The horseman of the first seal wears no diadem. The false crown is the stephanos. Its diamonds are paste. It is the shop girl adorned with jewelry from the ten-cent counter imitating the lady born and bred who wears the rich jewels of her inheritance. All is not gold that glitters. No amount of gaudy trappings can deceive the spiritual eye. Clothes do not make the man in spite of the proverb.[11]

Second, the four horses and their riders have an essential likeness to each other. The other three horsemen are all evil powers of tragedy and destruction. Christ cannot be put anywhere even in the same ballpark or on the same level as the other three horsemen.[12]

Third, Christ is the Lamb who is opening the seals in Revelation 6:1. He is the only one worthy to do so (5:2–8) and remains in control of their contents. It would be strange for Him to open the seal judgments and also constitute the contents of one of the seals.

Who then is this rider? If he is not military conquest, the proclamation of the gospel, or Christ Himself, then who is he? Clearly, he must be someone who closely resembles Christ, because like Christ he rides a white horse and wears a crown. The chief candidate, of course, is the Antichrist.

View #4:
The rider on the white horse is the Antichrist

There are two key points that strongly favor identifying this rider as the coming world dictator—the Antichrist.

First—and for me the most convincing evidence of this identification—are the incredible parallels between Matthew 24:4–14 and Revelation 6–7. The parallels are so close that Matthew 24 is often referred to as the "mini apocalypse," or miniature book of Revelation.

Viewing the four horsemen as parallel with Matthew 24:4–8 allows Jesus Himself to identify them. All four of the horsemen represent movements that will be at work in the end times. To be precise, then, the rider on the white horse is a movement or wave of false messiahs that will appear after the rapture

Matthew 24:4–14	Revelation 6–7
False Christs (vv. 4–5)	The Rider on the White Horse (vv. 1–2)
Wars and Rumors of Wars (24:6–7)	The Rider on the Red Horse (vv. 3–4)
Famines and Earthquakes (24:7b)	The Rider on the Black Horse (vv. 5–6)
Famines and Plagues (v. 7; Luke 21:11)	The Rider on the Pale Horse (vv. 7–8)
Persecution and Martyrdom (vv. 9–10)	Martyrs (vv. 9–11)
Terrors and Great Cosmic Signs (Luke 21:11)	Terror (vv. 12–17)
Worldwide Preaching of the Gospel (v. 14)	Ministry of the 144,000 (7:1–8)

of the church to heaven. The disappearance of the true believers will pave the way for an outbreak of counterfeit Christs, false messiahs who will claim to have the answers for the world's chaos. But out of this movement of false messiahs, one man will stand head and shoulders above the rest. He will be the ultimate fulfillment of the rider on the white horse, the ultimate anti-messiah. He will be the one who later, in Revelation 13:1–10, is called the beast out of the sea.

We know him best as the Antichrist.

Second, Revelation 6:2 says, "A crown was given to him." The verb *edothe* ("was given") is used repeatedly in Revelation of divine permission for evil forces to carry out their wicked plans (9:1, 3, 5; 13:5, 7, 14–15).[13] Notice that this term is used frequently in Revelation 13 to describe the source of this coming world ruler's power: It is given to him by God. This verb reminds the reader that God is in control and that all the events in Revelation are being directed from the throne of God. This notion of divine permission fits perfectly with the view that the rider on the white horse is the Antichrist.

As Billy Graham says, "Who, therefore, is the rider on the white horse? He is not Christ, but a deceiver who seeks to capture the hearts and souls of men and women. He is one who seeks to have people acknowledge him as Lord instead of the true Christ."[14]

David Jeremiah aptly calls this rider "the Dark Prince on a White Horse."[15]

He's the coming false messiah who will come forth to deceive the world and convince them that he's a man of peace. He will ride forth at the beginning of the Tribulation to bring peace in the midst of global upheaval and turmoil.

THE PEACEMAKER

Most people fail to realize that over one hundred passages in the Bible detail the origin, nationality, career, character, kingdom, and final doom of the Antichrist.

What do you think of when you hear the word *Antichrist?* A crazed madman? A diabolical fiend? A modern Adolf Hitler? A shameless egomaniac? While all of these images are accurate, none of them picture what Antichrist will be like when the world gets its first impression of him.

At the beginning of his career, the Antichrist will slip unobtrusively onto the stage of world events. The initial, clear mention of him in the Bible is in Daniel

7:8, where he is called "a little horn." His first appearance will be inconspicuous.

The first clue in Scripture as to the identity of Antichrist is found in Daniel 9:27, where he is pictured brokering a peace treaty with Israel: "And he [Antichrist] will make a firm covenant with the many for one week [seven years]." This means that when the world gets its first glimpse of Antichrist, it will be as a great peacemaker.

Charles Dyer, a respected prophecy teacher and author, writes:

> What is this "covenant" that the Antichrist will make with Israel? Daniel does not specify its content, but he does indicate that it will extend for seven years. During the first half of this time Israel feels at peace and secure, so the covenant must provide some guarantee for Israel's national security. Very likely the covenant will allow Israel to be at peace with her Arab neighbors. One result of the covenant is that Israel will be allowed to rebuild her temple in Jerusalem. This world ruler will succeed where Kissinger, Carter,

Reagan, Bush, and other world leaders have failed. He will be known as the man of peace![16]

Antichrist will come with the olive branch of peace in his hand. He will step on the scene and accomplish what generations had considered impossible. He will solve the Middle Eastern peace puzzle. He will rid the world of terrorism. He will be hailed as the greatest peacemaker who has ever lived. He will usher in a time of false peace at the dawn of the Tribulation—a mock millennium that will counterfeit the thousand-year reign of Christ predicted in Revelation 20:1–6.

Can't you just see it now? He will be *Time* magazine's Man of the Year. He will be interviewed on *60 Minutes*. He will capture the Nobel Peace Prize hands down.

BLOODLESS VICTORY

Revelation 6:2 describes the rider on the white horse as having a bow and wearing a crown. He wears a victor's crown and has a bow…but no arrows! This symbolism seems to indicate that he will win a bloodless victory at the beginning of his career. The bow indicates the threat of war, but it never materializes, because he is able to gain victory through peaceful negotiations.

He brings what the world wants more than anything else—worldwide peace and safety. We know that he ushers in a time of worldwide peace because the rider on the second horse in Revelation 6:3–4, the red horse, comes and takes peace from the earth. As we have noted, for peace to be taken from the earth it must first exist.

SATANIC SUPERMAN

You might be asking how the Antichrist will be able to pull this off. How will he do what so many other intelligent, committed statesmen have miserably failed to do? The answer is that he will be energized and empowered by Satan himself. He will have the full power of the evil one behind him like no man who has ever lived. Revelation 13:2 says, "And the dragon [Satan] gave him [Antichrist] his power and his throne and great authority."

Antichrist will possess all the qualities of all the great leaders who have ever lived rolled into one man. To help us better envision what the Antichrist will be like, H. L. Willmington, a noted Bible prophecy expert, has provided this helpful analogy with American presidents. The coming world ruler will possess:

- the leadership of a Washington and Lincoln
- the eloquence of a Franklin Roosevelt
- the charm of a Teddy Roosevelt
- the charisma of a Kennedy
- the popularity of an Ike
- the political savvy of a Johnson
- the intellect of a Jefferson[17]

Since he will be uniquely empowered by Satan, like his master he will masquerade as an angel of light, hiding his true goal of world domination. But at the midpoint of the Tribulation, the mask of peace will come off, and the world will be plunged into the terrible darkness of the Great Tribulation.

SHADOWS OF THE DARK PRINCE

Coming events almost always cast their shadows before them. And if we look at our world today, we can see shadows on the ground—shadows cast upon our own times by approaching apocalyptic events. The days of the Apocalypse have not yet dawned, but even today we can begin to see what that time of judgment will be like. The rider on the white horse is not abroad, but we can see the shadow of this horse on every hand. Our world today is perfectly prepared for the rider on the white horse to gallop onto the world scene.

There are no longer two key players in our planet's balance of power formula as there were from 1950–1990. Now, there seem to be dozens. The world is more at risk today for nuclear detonations and biological and chemical warfare than ever before. Pakistan and India have the bomb. So does China—and probably North Korea. Iran is coming perilously close. It's only a matter of time until rogue states, terrorists, or fanatics get their hands on these weapons of mass destruction. The foment in key Islamic nations could easily erupt into an explosive call for widespread jihad or holy war. The world is a more dangerous place than it's ever been at any point in human history—even in the days of the superpower standoff with the Soviet Empire.

The great need in our uncertain world today is peace and safety. People the world over are clamoring for peace—peace in the Balkans, peace in strife-torn African nations, but most of all, peace in the Middle East. We want a peaceful world in which to prosper and raise our families. During Operation Iraqi Freedom, millions in Europe flooded the streets of London and Rome in protest and calling for peace.

As Henry Morris points out, "Men have longed for peace. There have been peace treaties, disarmament conferences, leagues of nations, peace prizes, demonstrations for peace—all seeking somehow to bring in a lasting world peace. But all have failed."[18]

People are also yearning for safety. The world has become obsessed with security. We have never felt more unsafe, more exposed, more vulnerable, than we do right now. We want safety. Safety for ourselves. Safety for our children. Safety from a nuclear nightmare, safety from terrorist bombings, safety from bioterrorism, safety from chemical warfare. We want safe water, safe food, and safe air travel.

Of course, this longing is nothing new. But with the rise of war by stealth—the sudden, unexpected, mindless strike of terrorism—the cry for peace and safety has become a worldwide cadence.

Amazingly, the Bible predicts that someday the

world will finally achieve peace *and* safety. In 1 Thessalonians 5:3, the Scripture says that a day is coming when people everywhere will be saying, "All is well; everything is peaceful and secure" (NLT).

How will this ever be achieved? Frankly, right now it looks impossible. But the Bible says a man is coming who will bring it to pass. A man is coming who will give the world what it clamors for. The Bible calls this man by many names and titles.

And one of them is "the rider on the white horse" in Revelation 6:2.

SO WHAT'S HOLDING HIM BACK?

All that is keeping the rider on the white horse from riding across the earth is God's restraint by the power of the Holy Spirit through the church of Jesus Christ (2 Thessalonians 2:5–7). That's an incredible reality. *We* are the restrainer. You and I. The Spirit-indwelt church. And right now, the restrainer is still here and the seven-sealed scroll is still sealed.

But once that restrainer is removed at the Rapture, the Antichrist will ride forth to take his place on center stage. In his book *Escape the Coming Night,* David Jeremiah writes these arresting words:

The world is looking for a man on a white horse. Nations are churning. Revolutions are toppling governments. In this nuclear age, men live with the threat of international catastrophe. The final dictator, promising peace and prosperity, will be welcomed as the savior and hope of the world; he will command the military and mesmerize the masses. Governments will be united under his leadership and the people of the earth will sigh with relief, believing their future will be brighter.[19]

His grand entrance on the world stage may be very soon.

Can you hear the hoofbeats?

CHAPTER FOUR

THE BRINGER OF WAR

When General Dobey, British commander of Malta during World War I, was stationed in the Holy Land in 1916, an aide approached him and said, "Sir, this is a funny war we're fighting. The Muslims won't fight on Fridays, the Jews won't fight on Saturdays, and Christians won't fight on Sundays."

With Solomon-like wisdom, Dobey replied, "Well, if you can find four other world religions that refuse to fight on Monday, Tuesday, Wednesday, or Thursday because of their holy day, you have solved the problem of world peace."

That would be nice, wouldn't it? But we all know this is a dream. We live on a war-torn planet. Ever since Cain slew Abel, our planet has been plunged in strife, bloodshed, violence, and mayhem.

From 2,278 wars by the twelfth century, the total

increased to 13,835 in the first quarter of this century. Wilbur M. Smith estimated that "up to the close of the nineteenth century...14 billion people have been killed in the wars of the human race."

From 1496 B.C. to A.D. 1861, the world groaned under 3,130 years of war—relieved by less than 227 years of peace. Gustave Valbert reported that from 1500 B.C. to A.D. 1860, European nations have signed more than eight thousand peace treaties—each meant to remain in force forever. On average, they remained in force only two years. And just think of all the treaties that have been forged and broken since 1860!

In this century, 37.5 million died in World War I. An incredible 45.4 million died in World War II. In the Vietnam conflict, 57,605 U.S. lives were lost and 304,000 U.S. military personnel were injured.[20]

Let's face it. War is a terrible reality for our planet. As Plato once said, "Only the dead have seen the end of war." War will be a part of man's history until the Prince of Peace returns. Only when Jesus returns will the world find the peaceful utopia it has yearned for through the ages. But before Jesus comes, the Bible tells us that things on this earth will get worse before they get better. Much worse. Jesus said that one of the signs of His return to the earth will be warfare breaking out all over the globe.

> "You will be hearing of wars and rumors of wars. See that you are not frightened, for those things must take place, but that is not yet the end. For nation will rise against nation, and kingdom against kingdom." (Matthew 24:6–7)

The red horse of Revelation 6 will bring that devastation.

THE WAR HORSE

When the Lamb opens the second seal, John hears the summons from the second living being saying, "Come." Then the second horse thunders forth.

> When He broke the second seal, I heard the second living creature saying, "Come." And another, a red horse, went out; and to him who sat on it, it was granted to take peace from the earth, and that men would slay one another; and a great sword was given to him. (Revelation 6:3–4)

When John said he saw "another" horse, he used the Greek word *allos,* which normally means "another of the same kind." In other words, this horse and rider are of the same kind as the first one. It reveals a close connection between the two. Scholars agree almost universally that this horse and rider represent war, international strife, and civil war. The peace of the white horse is suddenly replaced by the war of the red horse.

Three key features identify the second horse and its rider: the color of the horse, the sword carried by the rider, and the activity of the horseman. All three of these features substantiate the identity of this rider with war.

SEEING RED

The second horse's color is described in the original Greek language as *pyrros* or "fiery red." The horse is as red as fire. The color, of course, illustrates the nature of the judgment under this seal. It depicts the awful horror of slaughter, bloodshed, and terror.

This is the same color (fiery red) as the great dragon in Revelation 12:3: "Then another sign appeared in heaven: and behold, a great red dragon having seven heads and ten horns, and on his heads were seven diadems." I can't help but see a connection here. The ultimate power behind the bloodshed and warfare is Satan himself. He hates humankind with a hatred that reaches all the way back to Eden. And he has been a murderer from the beginning (John 8:44; 1 John 3:12).

THE GREAT SWORD

Not only is the horse fiery red like blood, but the rider carries a great sword. In the Greek, it's a *mega machaira*. Sometimes in Greek *machaira* refers to a short knife carried in a sheath at the girdle (John 18:10). But other times it refers to the long sword carried in battle by Roman soldiers. The addition of the word *mega* (great) before the word *machaira* undoubtedly indicates that the long Roman sword is in view here.[21]

So here we see a bloodred horse with a rider wielding a huge Roman broadsword.

TAKING PEACE FROM THE EARTH

Revelation 6:4 says that the rider on the red horse will take peace from the earth. But to be more specific and accurate, the verse actually says, "it was granted to take *the* peace from the earth." In the Greek, the definite article *the* is in front of the word *peace*.

Why is this significant? What is *the* peace that this rider will snatch away from the earth? The best interpretation is that this refers to the world-wide peace ushered in by the rider on the white horse.

What this tells us, then, is that by means of the red horse, God will interrupt man's pseudo peace with the outpouring of His wrath and the outbreak of war. Referring to this same period of time, 1 Thessalonians 5:3 says, "While they are saying, 'Peace and safety!' then destruction will come upon them suddenly like labor pains upon a woman with child, and they will not escape."

Man's utopia under the Antichrist won't last long. Antichrist's promised peace is brief and illusory. God will bring it to an abrupt end with the opening of the second seal judgment in Revelation 6:3–4. When the rider on the red horse gallops forth with a mighty sword in his hand, much of the world will be plunged into war and slaughter. Israel will continue to enjoy peace for the first three and a half years of the Tribulation, until she is invaded by Antichrist (see Daniel 11:40–45), but most of the world will begin to experience what Jesus predicted in Matthew 24:6–7:

"You will be hearing of wars and rumors of wars. See that you are not frightened, for those things must take place, but that is not yet the end. For nation will rise against nation, and kingdom against kingdom."

So much for man's ability to bring peace to the world by his own efforts.

THE ROAD TO ARMAGEDDON

The world today is a powder keg. The Korean peninsula. Liberia. Israel and the Palestinians. Iraq. India versus Pakistan. The Balkans. Rogue states like Iran. Terrorists.

It doesn't take a great imagination to see how war could break out all over the world. When the rider on the red horse rides forth, the dam will break—releasing a reservoir of blood and fury. The brief respite from war will shatter like a pane of thin glass, and men everywhere will "slay one another" (6:4). It will be like nothing the world has ever seen, with modern weapons of mass destruction undoubtedly playing a key role in the scope of the devastation. In just the last few decades, man has come up with more and better weapons and delivery systems to kill his fellow man by the millions—and even billions.

Nuclear weapons.

Chemical weapons.

Biological weapons.

And the development of these weapons continues at an alarming rate. These weapons point toward the coming of the red horse. The stage is set. As Billy Graham noted:

> Jesus indicated that when this type of war does come to pass (Matthew 24:22), "If those days had not been cut short, no one would survive." This refers to total war, with the annihilation of all mankind as a probable outcome—barring divine intervention. Never before has total cos-mocide—world death—been at men's finger-tips. There are no precedents in political science or in human history to guide the men who command modern power. Mankind may have always had war, but never on the scale that Jesus predicted in Matthew 24 and Revelation 6. Never before has man had the potential to totally obliterate the human race.[22]

The red horse will bathe the earth in blood.

And what begins with the rider on the red horse during the first half of the seven-year Tribulation will continue and intensify during the ghastly final three and a half years. All of this hatred and bloodshed will continue to build until man's inhumanity to man climaxes in the final great war of this age—the campaign of Armageddon.

The rider on the red horse may be saddling up even now.

CHAPTER FIVE

THE BLACK STALLION

In the Museum of Modern Art in New York City, Umberto Boccioni's *The City Rises* portrays the four horsemen of the Apocalypse in a modern, urban setting. The oil painting occupies a massive six-foot-six-inch by nine-foot-ten-inch canvas. It singles out the horror of the third horse and its rider. Boccioni depicts the black horse as a tornado, spinning wildly above the other horsemen.[23]

What an apt depiction. The black horse will whirl forth, leaving a devastating debris field in its wake.

Having lived in central Oklahoma for over forty years, I know something about the devastation of tornadoes. I live in "tornado alley." In fact, just an hour before I wrote these words, I personally witnessed the damage from an F-4 tornado that tracked within five miles of my house a few days ago.

Boccioni had it right. The black stallion and its rider portend terrible ruin for the world.

THE BLACK HORSE OF WANT

As the third seal is broken in Revelation 6:5–6, the jet-black horse gallops across the globe in the horrific wake of the first two horsemen. The apostle John recorded what he saw:

> When He broke the third seal, I heard the third living creature saying, "Come." I looked, and behold, a black horse; and he who sat on it had a pair of scales in his hand. And I heard something like a voice in the center of the four living creatures saying, "A quart of wheat for a denarius, and three quarts of barley for a denarius; and do not damage the oil and the wine."

The third horse is black as midnight. Black as tar. The mere color itself signals something ominous, dark, and dreadful. But what do this horse and rider represent? Although there have been several different suggestions for the identity of this horse and rider, they clearly personify famine and hunger. The black color undoubtedly signifies the lamentation and sorrow of extreme deprivation.

Four points favor this identification of the black horse and its rider.

First, after the red horse and the outbreak of war, food shortages cannot be far behind. This is the way it has always been. Hunger is one of the wretched results of war.

Second, the identification is confirmed by the parallel with Jesus' list of end-time signs in Matthew 24:7, as we have already seen. According to Jesus, the first three birth pangs of the end times are false messiahs, war, and famine. As we have seen, this tracks parallel with the horsemen in Revelation 6:1–8.

Third, the color black often signifies the haunting specter of hunger. For instance, Lamentations 4:8–9 says, "Their appearance is blacker than soot, they are not recognized in the streets; their skin is shriveled on their bones, it is withered, it has become like wood. Better are those slain with the sword than those slain with hunger; for they pine away, being stricken for lack of the fruits of the field."

Fourth (and the clincher) is the fact that the rider

holds a pair of scales in his hand. This refers to a bar with scales at both ends—or some kind of weight at one end with a pan suspended at the other.[24] In Revelation 6:5, the rider is carefully weighing food on the scales: "And he who sat on it had a pair of scales in his hand." This activity reveals that food is in short supply. Consuming food in carefully-weighed-out portions is a sign of famine (Ezekiel 4:16–17).

The haunting phantom of famine rides forth.

THE VOICE OF GOD

While John is mesmerized by the black horse and rider with scales in his hand, he suddenly hears an unidentified voice coming from "the center of the four living creatures" saying, "A quart of wheat for a denarius and three quarts of barley for a denarius; and do not damage the oil and the wine" (Revelation 6:6). This is unusual. This is the only time with any of the four horsemen that a voice speaks, other than the living creature who announces the coming of each horse and rider.

Who is this speaking?

Several different answers have been given. Some believe this is Jesus, the Lamb, speaking. After all, He is One who is opening these seals that bring forth the judgment of the four horsemen. But it seems even stronger to identify this voice with God the Father, seated on His throne and surrounded by the four living creatures (Revelation 4:6–8). If this is correct, then God, enthroned in majesty and splendor, is breaking into the narrative to add His sovereign commentary on the severity of the coming judgment.

This cry of the Almighty from His throne makes this coming world famine even more ominous. The black rider is very black indeed.

FAMINE IN THE LAND

I don't know if you've ever been hungry before. I mean really hungry—with that deep gnawing hunger in the pit of your stomach. When you would eat about anything you could get your hands on.

For four years, I worked for Judge Hez Bussey on the Oklahoma Court of Criminal Appeals. He survived the Bataan death march and three and a half years in Japanese concentration camps. When the Japanese surrendered in 1945, the judge, who was about five foot ten, weighed 103 pounds. He said that if the war had lasted a few more weeks, he would not have made it. He used to tell me stories about eating bugs or worms—anything he could get his hands on. He told me once about a group of hungry prisoners on a work detail leaping on a snake in the water and carving it up into pieces in a matter of seconds. His fingernails were disfigured from having bamboo shoots jammed underneath them during a Japanese interrogation concerning some stolen rice. He and a few other men had stolen the rice at the risk of their lives, but they didn't give in to the interrogators, even under merciless torture.

The average American knows nothing about going hungry. I know I don't. My idea of a fast is the time between lunch and dinner. Sadly, we have the opposite problem in our country. I read recently that 65 percent of Americans are overweight. About one in three is obese—that is, at least one hundred pounds over their ideal body weight. We live in the land of plenty, and we should be deeply thankful for this tremendous blessing from God. But let's face it—way too many of us spend way too much time in the pantry and refrigerator. We eat for entertainment and fun. There's an abundance of scrumptious food all around us.

According to the Bible, however, it's not always

going to be this way. The black horse of famine is on the horizon. Before his ride is complete, the whole world will be like one giant concentration camp, desperate just to find some morsel to bring momentary relief.

How bad will it be? Revelation 6:6 gives us a glimpse at just two of the devastating consequences of this famine.

1. Terrible inflation

During the famine of the Tribulation period, it will take a denarius to buy a measure of wheat or three measures of barley. A denarius in that day was a silver coin equal to the average day's wages for a working man. A measure *(koinix)* or "quart" of grain in the first century was equal to slightly less than our modern quart. And one measure or quart of wheat was the basic portion of food for one person for one day. What this indicates is that the purchasing power of a denarius will drop far below what is normal. In other words, the world will experience runaway inflation. Food prices will be so high that it will take everything a person can earn just to buy enough food for one meal. The prices listed here are eight to sixteen times the average prices in the Roman Empire at the time John wrote.

As John Walvoord wrote: "To put it in ordinary language, the situation would be such that one would have to spend a day's wages for a loaf of bread with no money left to buy anything else. The symbolism therefore indicates a time of famine when life will be reduced to the barest necessities."[25]

2. Degenerating food quality

With the world economy suffering runaway inflation, the kind of food people can afford will quickly degenerate. Since it will take all a person can earn in a day just to buy enough regular food for one person for one day, people will resort to lower quality food just to put something on the table for their families.

Wheat was the main food of the ancient world. Barley was a lesser quality grain with less nutritional value, often used to feed animals. During the future famine of the end times, people will quit buying the normal foods they have been used to and will turn to cheaper foods. By eating food of grossly inferior quality, a family of three could eat three meals a day of barley, whereas they could only eat one meal of wheat.

To put this in today's market perspective, it will take all the money a man or woman can earn in a day just to buy meat and potatoes for one person for one day *or* macaroni and cheese or beans to feed a whole family for a day.

The world will be consumed by the rider on the black horse. Earth will writhe in the clutches of stabbing hunger.

LIFESTYLES OF THE
RICH AND FAMOUS

Revelation 6:6 makes clear that the famine that breaks out during the first half of the Tribulation will not be universal. One group will be exempt from this horror. As the masses endure runaway inflation and degenerating food quality, the wealthy will enjoy a temporary exemption from this time of judgment. Verse 6b adds, "and do not damage the oil and the wine." This means that while the basic staples for life are being decimated, the oil and wine will go untouched. And in that day, oil and wine were more in the categories of luxury than wheat and barley.[26]

During the coming Tribulation, the gulf between rich and poor will grow even wider. Food will be so expensive that only the wealthy will have enough. Famine will relentlessly hammer the middle and lower classes. The vast majority will be wallowing in misery, but the rich will continue to bask in the comforts of their luxurious lifestyle. The wealthy will continue to flourish. They will not only have the necessities of life, but will still enjoy the luxuries as well. This will make the suffering of the masses even more unbearable as they watch the privileged few indulge themselves in the lap of luxury.[27]

I don't know about you, but to me this looks unfair. Why will the rich be exempt from God's judgment? Is God playing favorites? Not at all. The rich will escape this first wave of judgment, but as the Tribulation moves along, they too will cry out in despair. The rich will not escape God's judgment for long. Under the sixth seal judgment in Revelation 6:15–17, the wealthy will suffer the heavy hand of God's wrath.

> Then the kings of the earth and the great men and the commanders and the rich and the strong and every slave and free man hid themselves in the caves and among the rocks of the

mountains; and they said to the mountains and to the rocks, "Fall on us and hide us from the presence of Him who sits on the throne, and from the wrath of the Lamb; for the great day of their wrath has come; and who is able to stand?"

The old poem by Friedrich von Logau will be amply fulfilled:

Though the mills of God grind slowly,
Yet they grind exceeding small;
Though with patience He stands waiting,
With exactness grinds He all.

WHAT CAN I DO NOW?

The rider on the black horse has not come forth yet. The Tribulation period has not begun. The church of Jesus Christ is still here, holding out the Word of Life and the promise of salvation to all who will respond, offering help and hope and healing to those who have been bruised and crushed and left behind in our world's headlong rush for pleasure and power.

We are still here. And we ought to ask ourselves what God would have us do as we await His coming and our Rapture into His presence. What would the black horse say to us today?

How easy it is today for those of us in affluent Western nations to turn a deaf ear to the harsh reality of hunger in much of the world. If you're like me, when you think of hungry people around the world, the first thought that comes to mind is, *What can I do? After all, I'm just one person, and the problem is so overwhelming.* But if each of us would stretch ourselves even a little, we could provide help for the emaciated masses who are enduring the horror of famine right now.

As we await the coming of Christ, may God help us do all we can to alleviate suffering around the world—and even in our own nation. One in six children in America does not get proper nourishment. This hits pretty close to home, doesn't it? Find a family to help. Get your church involved in helping the helpless in your community.

James 1:27 is an apt reminder for us about what God says is true religion in His eyes: "Pure and undefiled religion in the sight of our God and Father is this:

to visit orphans and widows in their distress, and to keep oneself unstained by the world."

May our "religion" be true and genuine in the eyes of God as we await the coming of our blessed Savior.

CHAPTER SIX

PALE RIDER

I'm not sure why, but I love cowboy and western movies. Maybe it's because I grew up in Oklahoma. Who knows? By far, my favorites are the ones starring Clint Eastwood. I'm talking about classics like *Hang 'Em High, The Outlaw Josey Wales, High Plains Drifter,* and *Unforgiven.* (As you can tell, I'm a person of great culture.)

My wife and sons can't understand why I've memorized lines from so many of the Eastwood westerns. They just shake their heads.

In 1985, Clint Eastwood starred as a mysterious preacher who rides into a mining town that is being oppressed by a local mine owner. The movie is called *Pale Rider.*

Near the beginning of the movie, a teenage girl is sitting in her cabin with her mother doing her morning Bible reading. The text for the morning is Revelation 6:6–8. The girl slowly reads the sobering words describing the final horseman of the Apocalypse —the pale rider.

As the words are coming out of her mouth, she peers out the window and sees Clint Eastwood, riding into town on a pale horse. Predictably, as the movie unfolds, the preacher is good in a fight and quick on the draw. In the end, he stands up against the mine owner and his hired posse of fast guns. The movie ends with the preacher on the pale horse mysteriously disappearing into the distant horizon. (Don't you just love it?)

Clint Eastwood's character in this movie is steely-eyed and tough. He leaves devastation in his path if people mess with him.

But he is nothing compared to the pale rider who is coming: the fourth of the apocalyptic horsemen.

DEATHLY PALE

After detailing the terrible devastation wrought by the first three riders, John describes the final horse in the corral:

> When the Lamb broke the fourth seal, I heard the voice of the fourth living creature saying, "Come." I looked, and behold, an ashen

horse; and he who sat on it had the name Death; and Hades was following with him. Authority was given to them over a fourth of the earth, to kill with sword and with famine and with pestilence and by the wild beasts of the earth. (Revelation 6:7–8)

The word used to describe the fourth horse's color is *ashen.* The Greek word for the horse's color is *chloros*—from which we derive our English word *chlorine.* Chloros usually denotes a pale green color and is used elsewhere in Revelation to describe the color of grass and vegetation (8:7; 9:4).

In Revelation 6:8, it pictures the color of a decomposing corpse.

Robert Thomas describes the grotesque color of the fourth horse as "the yellowish green of decay, the pallor of death. It is the pale ashen color that images a face bleached because of terror. It recalls a corpse in the advanced state of corruption."[28]

THE FACE OF DEATH

The fourth horse and rider have two unique features that distinguish them from the others. First, the name of the rider is given. We aren't left to wonder about his identity.

What's his name? *Death*. The most feared name in the world. The thing that all men avoid at all cost.

In his story *The Appointment in Samara,* W. Somerset Maugham emphasizes man's fear of death and its dreadful inevitability. He tells of a certain merchant in Baghdad who sent his servant to the market to buy some provisions. A little while later, the servant returned, looking white in the face. In a trembling voice he said, "Just now in the marketplace I was jostled by a man in the crowd, and when I turned I saw it was Mr. Death. He looked at me and made a threatening gesture. Please lend me your horse, because I want to go to Samara where Mr. Death will not be able to find me."

The merchant agreed and lent the terrified man his horse. The servant mounted the horse and rode away as fast as the animal could gallop. Later that day, the merchant went down to the marketplace and saw Mr. Death standing in the crowd. He approached him and said, "Why did you make a threatening gesture to my servant when you saw him this morning?"

"That was not a threatening gesture," said Mr.

Death. "It was only a start of surprise. I was astonished to see him in Baghdad, because I have an appointment with him tonight in Samara."

The fourth horseman is the fearful face of death. The grim reaper.

HELL ON HIS HEELS

The second unique feature of the fourth horseman is his shadow. Wherever the horseman rides, he is followed by Hades. In the Greek New Testament, the word *Hades* appears ten times. From these uses, we discover that Hades is the part of the underworld or netherworld where the souls of lost people are presently confined while they await the final day of judgment. At the final judgment, they will be cast into *Gehenna,* or the lake of fire, as their permanent abode for all eternity.

Here in Revelation 6, Hades is personified. Hades trails along behind the pale horse. Whether Hades is also mounted or is on foot isn't stated. Somehow, it seems appropriate that he would be on foot. As Death stampedes across the earth, Hades follows closely behind to swallow up the helpless victims strewn in his terrible wake.[29]

THE DAY A BILLION PEOPLE
WILL DIE

The death rider will bring unimaginable carnage. The world will be littered with the carcasses of his victims. Hades will have a field day—and this is no exaggeration. Let these words soak in: "Authority was given to them over a fourth of the earth, to kill" (Revelation 6:8).

One-fourth of the world's population will die at the hands of the pale rider. That's over 1 billion people. Earth's current population stands at about 6 billion. Let's assume generously that 1 billion people disappear at the rapture of the church to heaven. That will leave at least 5 billion souls to enter the time of Tribulation. And one-fourth of 5 billion is over a billion people.

The entire population of the United States in the 2000 census was 282 million. It takes almost four of the United States to equal 1 billion—about the entire population of either China or India.

Gone in one Tribulation judgment.

Swept away.

And as fearsome as this judgment is, we have to remember that Jesus called this event merely one of the beginning birth pangs of the Tribulation: "For nation will rise against nation, and kingdom against kingdom, and in various places there will be famines and earthquakes. But all these things are merely the beginning of birth pangs" (Matthew 24:7–8).

The worst will still be yet to come. Another one-third of the earth will later die in the fifth trumpet judgment (Revelation 9:18).

But how will God do it? How will He destroy one-fourth of the world's population?

Four Dreadful Judgments

The Bible says that the fourth horseman named Death will use four means to wreak his havoc.

> Authority was given to them over a fourth of the earth, to kill with sword and with famine and with pestilence and by the wild beasts of the earth. (Revelation 6:8)

The first means that the final rider has at his disposal is the sword. Again, just as with the second seal, this clearly refers to warfare that will continue to intensify and take its toll of lives as the Tribulation rolls on. Millions will die as the earth is overrun with bloody wars.

The second means of death is famine. This is

reminiscent of the third seal. The famine introduced by the black horse will mushroom as its dark veil shrouds the earth.

The third means of death for one-fourth of the earth's population is described as "pestilence." Actually, in the original Greek the word is *thanato*, which most often simply means "death." In this case, however, it probably refers to death by means of pestilence, plague, or disease. Sword, famine, and pestilence are frequently associated with one another in the Old Testament (1 Chronicles 21:12; Jeremiah 14:12; 21:7; 24:10; 44:13; Ezekiel 5:12; 6:11–12). For that matter, Jesus' blueprint of end-time signs in Luke 21:11 lists "plagues" as one of the final judgments: "And there will be great earthquakes, and in various places plagues and famines."[30]

Ezekiel 14:21 mentions the very same four judgments listed in Revelation 6:8. The prophet calls them God's "four severe judgments": "For thus says the Lord GOD, 'How much more when I send My four severe judgments against Jerusalem: sword, famine, wild beasts and plague to cut off man and beast from it!'" In the Greek translation of the Old Testament, Ezekiel 14:21 uses the same word for "pestilence" or "disease"—*thanato*—as Revelation 6:8.

The fourth way the rider on his pale mount will destroy is by "the wild beasts of the earth" (v. 8). As you might imagine, this reference has generated some diverse opinions. There are three main views on the identity of these wild beasts. First, it's possible that this refers to actual wild animals that will become especially ferocious during the Tribulation, as their normal food supplies are disrupted. They will look for prey and take advantage of the defenseless as God uses them to terrorize and destroy.[31] To borrow a line from *The Wizard of Oz,* it will be "lions and tigers and bears! Oh my!"

Another view is that "the wild beasts of the earth" is a reference to military and political leaders who subjugate and persecute their subjects, much like we have seen in the killing fields of Cambodia, in the purges of Mao, and most recently in the reign of terror of the Iraqi madman, Saddam Hussein. This view is based on the fact that the same word "wild beast," which in the Greek is *theerion,* is used thirty-eight times in Revelation, and every other time refers to the coming Antichrist or his henchman, the false prophet. This word is used to graphically express the vicious, brutal, bestial character of the Antichrist's kingdom. The word *theerion* occurs most frequently in Revelation 13, which presents these two "wild beasts" who rise to power in the end times to afflict the world.[32]

A third view is that the wild beasts are a reference to animals—but perhaps not the ones we would normally think of. John Phillips suggests that the "wild beasts" here in Revelation 6:8 might actually be that most deadly of all creatures—the rat!

> The beasts are closely linked with pestilence, and that might be a clue. The most destructive creature on earth, so far as mankind is concerned, is not the lion or the bear, but the rat. The rat is clever, adaptable, and destructive. If 95 percent of the rat population is exterminated in a given area, the rat population will replace itself within a year. It has killed more people than all the wars in history, and it makes its home wherever man is found. Rats carry as many as thirty-five different diseases. Their fleas carry bubonic plague, which killed a third of the population of Europe in the fourteenth century. Their fleas also carry typhus, which in four centuries has killed an

estimated 200 million people. Beasts, in this passage, are linked not only with pestilence, but with famine. Rats menace human food supplies, which they both devour and contaminate, especially in the more underdeveloped countries that can least afford to suffer loss.[33]

In my opinion, the best reading of "wild beasts" is in reference to vicious, brutal world political and military rulers—just the way the term is used every other time in the book of Revelation. But whichever view is correct, these wild beasts will play a prominent and deadly role in the four-fold devastation of the pale rider.

So, we can see that the four horsemen are kind of like a chain reaction. The first horse brings the Antichrist on the scene. The red horse that follows ushers in a time of war and bloodshed. War brings its inevitable result—the black horse of famine. Famine produces disease and death. And after death comes Hades and judgment.[34]

END-TIME PLAGUES

Before we leave our look at this fourth horseman, I want to pause and point out why I believe our world today is prepared like never before for the pale rider to make his appearance.

Just think about it. Our world is certainly ripe for a brutal bloodletting and the famine that will inevitably follow. But most significantly, our world is ripe for sweeping plagues of unparalleled scope. There are signs today that point toward these global plagues that will kill millions—or even billions—during the end times.

In the 1970s, scientists believed they had pretty much ended the day of sweeping killer microbes. But all that optimism ended in the early 1980s, when a strange new disease began to crop up. Before long it was identified by four letters...AIDS.

Every year on December 1, the world's attention is focused on AIDS in what is known as World AIDS Day. And the news about this modern-day plague is bleak. A new United Nations report says that there have been more deaths and infections worldwide in 2003 than ever before. The numbers are staggering. Three million people died of AIDS in 2003 alone.

Pause and let that sink in. That's about the same number as the entire population of my home state of Oklahoma. The AIDS death odometer is spinning at a rate of eight thousand people per day, and it continues to accelerate. And in 2003 alone, another 5 million people acquired human immunodeficiency virus (HIV). That brings the total number of people in the world living with HIV to about 42 million. The cost of treating this epidemic is $15 billion annually according to the United Nations. From the beginning of this epidemic to the end of 2001, the total number of AIDS orphans has soared to over fourteen million.[35]

In many African nations, AIDS is a weapon of mass destruction. When a sizable portion of the population becomes infected and can't work, the economy begins to fall apart, and chaos ensues. That national chaos can easily be exploited, and these nations can become international threats to stability and security—with far-reaching effects.

And while AIDS is by far the most serious plague, unfortunately it isn't the only problem out there. According to a recent *Newsweek* article, "How Progress Makes Us Sick," thirty new diseases have cropped up since the midseventies, causing tens of millions of deaths. The parade of frightening new maladies keeps marching on.

There's Ebola, mad cow disease, hantavirus, Avian

flu, Lyme disease, West Nile virus, SARS, and the list goes on and on. In late 2003, a serious strain of flu identified as H3N2 hit the central U.S. with the potential, according to experts, to kill seventy thousand people in the U.S. alone. The flu virus has changed its DNA many times. Another epidemic could occur at any time. Many experts are expecting an impending flu pandemic and cite lack of medicines as a major problem.

The Institute of Medicine says flatly, "Infectious diseases will continue to emerge."[36] Some of this is due to the emergence of new drug-resistant "super-bugs." There was a 58 percent rise in infectious disease deaths between 1980 and 1992, which many attribute to drug resistance.

And add to all this the man-made biological weapons containing smallpox, anthrax, Ebola, and who knows what else. These WMDs could wipe out hundreds of millions of people in a very short time. The devastation is too staggering even to think about.

I don't believe that any of these diseases today are the direct fulfillment of the Bible prophecies in Luke 21:11 or Revelation 6:8, but they do strikingly fore-shadow what lies ahead for planet earth during the dreadful days of the end. Decades ago, it was very difficult to have global plagues that would kill millions around the world. With lack of global travel, diseases were pretty much contained within limited geographical areas. Black Death, or the bubonic plague, hit Europe in 1347–1350. Interestingly, it was born in China and spread along trade routes. But it did its darkest work in Europe, where about twenty-five million perished. The Italian writer Boccaccio said its victims often "ate lunch with their friends and dinner with their ancestors in paradise."

The Black Death is an example of a plague that did spread somewhat, but was still relatively confined geographically.

But all that has changed dramatically in the last thirty years. Rapid means of world travel have interconnected the world population into a one-world community. This provides the perfect environment for plagues to spread quickly around the world, causing the extent of devastation predicted in Revelation 6:7–8.

The recent SARS outbreak is a perfect example. In a matter of weeks, the disease spread from China and Hong Kong to 4,800 cases in twenty-seven countries on six continents, resulting in 293 deaths. Even Toronto, Canada, known for its pristine environment, was declared a hazard to public health by the World Health Organization. How did this all happen so quickly? Why do diseases spread so quickly today?

The answer is simple: megacities, jet planes, factory farms, and blood banks. Just think: The Spanish flu killed twenty million people in eighteen months in 1918–1919. Its rapid spread and worldwide influence was very unusual for that day, when world travel was slow and expensive. The spread of the flu was probably related to troops from WWI going home and spreading the virus all over the world. But what if the same kind of virulent virus hit our global village today with its crowded, mobile population? It would be dispersed worldwide in no time.

Make no mistake—our world is ripe for the pale rider. The stage could not be more perfectly set for the fourth horseman to begin his ride. Things aren't looking very promising for the late, great planet earth, are they?

But before you give up hope, keep reading.

The best is yet to come! God has already given away the ending…and Jesus wins.

CHAPTER SEVEN

THE FIFTH HORSEMAN OF THE APOCALYPSE

Events in our world are converging with every passing hour, paving the way for the entrance of the four fearsome riders.

But before we bring together all the signs that point toward the sound of thundering hoofbeats, let's turn for a moment from darkness…to Light. From the Tribulation of man to the triumph of the Lord Jesus Christ. Focusing on the four horsemen for too long could make a person wonder if there is any hope—any light at the end of the Tribulation tunnel. But let's not forget to lift up our heads and see that the book of Revelation—above all else—is a book of hope, victory, and salvation. It's a majestic, messianic, moving book.

It is the revelation of Jesus Christ.

The King of kings and Lord of lords.

The Lamb upon the throne.

The Desire of all nations.

And He, too, comes forth from heaven riding on a horse. We might call Him the *fifth* horseman of the Apocalypse—the only hope for our lives and this dark world.

THE HEAVENLY HORSEMAN

John declares the theme of Revelation at the beginning of the book:

> Behold, He is coming with the clouds, and every eye will see Him, even those who pierced Him; and all the tribes of the earth will mourn over Him. So it is to be. Amen. (1:7)

Jesus Christ is coming back again. To earth. And every eye will see Him as He reenters the atmosphere of our world in power and great glory to establish His kingdom.

Revelation 19:11–18 is the climax of the book that records John's vision of that great event we call the Second Coming, when Jesus returns to earth to rule and reign in righteousness and wisdom...the great heavenly Conqueror charging from heaven on a milk-white stallion, as the great Warrior-Judge of the earth.

> And I saw heaven opened, and behold, a white horse, and He who sat on it is called Faithful and True, and in righteousness He judges and wages war. His eyes are a flame of fire, and on His head are many diadems; and He has a name written on Him which no one knows except Himself. He is clothed with a robe dipped in blood, and His name is called The Word of God. And the armies which are in heaven, clothed in fine linen, white and clean, were following Him on white horses. From His mouth comes a sharp sword, so that with it He may strike down the nations, and He will rule them with a rod of iron; and He treads the wine press of the fierce wrath of God, the Almighty. And on His robe and on His thigh He has a name written, "KING OF KINGS, AND LORD OF LORDS."
>
> Then I saw an angel standing in the sun, and he cried out with a loud voice, saying to all the birds which fly in midheaven, "Come,

assemble for the great supper of God, so that you may eat the flesh of kings and the flesh of commanders and the flesh of mighty men and the flesh of horses and of those who sit on them and the flesh of all men, both free men and slaves, and small and great."

In every sense, Jesus is the fifth and final horseman of the Apocalypse. He has the final word. He reverses all the terrible judgments of the four horsemen. He defeats the Antichrist. He brings an end to war. He stops the scourge of famine. He brings healing to the nations.

THE CELESTIAL CAVALRY

But Jesus won't be alone on that majestic ride!

Did you notice the words in Revelation 19:14? "And the armies which are in heaven, clothed in fine linen, white and clean, were following Him on white horses."

Jesus Christ won't be the only one on a white horse! He will be followed by a great army from heaven riding on white horses.

Who are these heavenly horsemen that ride with Christ?

Some believe they are angels. It is clear in the Bible that the angelic host will attend Christ at His Second Coming (Matthew 13:41; 16:27; 24:30–31; Mark 8:38; Luke 9:36; 2 Thessalonians 1:7). But for three reasons, it seems better to identify these riders following their King in Revelation 19 as His redeemed church.

First, notice that the riders are "clothed in fine linen" (Revelation 19:14). Just a few verses earlier, in verse 8, the fine linen is the clothing of the Lamb's bride, a reference to the church of Jesus Christ.

Second, in 17:14, those who return with Christ at His Second Coming, when He makes war against the Antichrist and his armies, are referred to as "the called and chosen and faithful." The text says, "These will wage war against the Lamb, and the Lamb will overcome them, because He is Lord of lords and King of kings, and those who are with Him are the called and chosen and faithful." This seems to clearly mark out the riders with Christ from heaven as God's saints, who will return with Him at His Second Coming.

Third, Revelation 2:27 tells us that the saints will rule the earth—with Christ—wielding a rod of iron. This is precisely what Jesus will do when He returns (19:15).

I can guess what you might be thinking at this point. *Is this army of white horses picture* real? *Is this literal—or just more symbolism? Will we* really *ride on celestial steeds as we return to earth with Christ?* This isn't an easy issue to decide, and certainly one should not be dogmatic about it either way. Clearly, some of the things in the surrounding context are symbolic—such as the sword coming out of Christ's mouth that symbolizes His spoken word. It also appears that the fine linen clothing of the saints is symbolic, since Revelation 19:8 identifies these garments as the "righteous acts of the saints."

As we have already noted, a white horse in that day symbolized victory and conquest. For that matter, the four horses in Revelation 6:1–8 are not literal horses that will ride across the earth. They are symbolic of great judgments that will sweep the earth.

On the other hand, much in the context *is* literal—the opening of heaven, the descent of Christ, and the terrible destruction that falls upon the earth. It is very possible that God may intend for us to take these horses literally. After all, God can create any kind of divinely energized creatures He chooses.[37] I lean toward the view that these are real celestial horses, created by God for His heavenly army to ride. (And please don't assume that this is only because I have a fondness for westerns!)

Nevertheless, either way you view these white horses, the point is clear. They speak of a great victory and homecoming that will literally take place upon the earth when Jesus returns.[38] It is a victory we will be part of if we have put our faith and trust in Jesus Christ as our Savior and Lord. And what a glorious day that will be!

An Army of One

When Christ descends from heaven, He will be ready for war. He's not coming back as a babe in the manger or a quiet carpenter or "gentle Jesus, meek and mild." He's coming back as the great Warrior-Messiah.

He triumphantly straddles a white horse. He wields a sword.

In stark contrast to the King, isn't it interesting how the armies following Christ are described in Revelation 19:14? All it says is that we are "clothed in fine linen, white and clean…on white horses."

Notice that we have no weapons. No swords, spears, or bows.

We wear no armor. And why should we? We are *immortal*—immune to even the slightest injury.

We take no part whatsoever in the action. We are support personnel only. Noncombatants. We come not to fight by His side but to reign with Him.

Christ will wage war all by Himself.[39] He will single-handedly wipe out the armies of the world led by Antichrist, who are gathered at Armageddon (Revelation 19:17–19). Jesus will slay them with the breath of His mouth (Isaiah 11:4; 2 Thessalonians 2:8). All He will have to do is say "Drop dead" and it will all be over. But this doesn't necessarily mean there will be no bloodshed associated with Messiah's conquest. Other passages in the Bible reveal that Christ will slaughter His enemies when He returns to earth (Isaiah 34:1–6; 63:1–3; Revelation 14:19–20). Christ's coming will be a bloodbath for His enemies.

Make no mistake. We will descend from heaven with Christ. But He alone is the Conqueror.

One of the specific things Jesus will do at His return is cast the Antichrist and false prophet alive into the lake of fire: "And the beast was seized, and with him the false prophet who performed the signs in his presence, by which he deceived those who had received the mark of the beast and those who worshiped his image; these two were thrown alive into the lake of fire which burns with brimstone" (Revelation 19:20).

The final rider on the white horse, the true Messiah, will take the psuedo Christ and cast him alive into the lake of fire. He and his sidekick, the false prophet, will be the first two inhabitants of that unthinkably horrible place.

I think it's fitting that Antichrist, the counterfeit Christ, who rides on a white horse at the beginning of the Tribulation to set up his world kingdom, is defeated by the second rider on a white horse at the end of the Tribulation, who comes to establish His glorious kingdom on the earth, which will last for one thousand years.

WHAT GOES UP MUST COME DOWN

A Christian woman was once telling a pastor about the assurance of her salvation. She said, "I have a one-way ticket to glory and don't intend to come back." To this the man of God replied, "Well, you're sure going to miss a lot. I have taken a round-trip ticket. I'm not only going to meet Christ in glory, but I'm coming back with Him in power and great glory to earth."

Every believer in Christ in the present church age has a round-trip ticket. The fact that those who have trusted Jesus as their Savior will *descend* with Christ from heaven at His Second Coming means that at some time before that coming we must have gone *up* to heaven. Right? It only makes sense. We can't come back with Him from heaven if we haven't gone up to heaven in the first place.

But when will we go up?

I believe that we will be caught up, or raptured, to heaven before the beginning of the seven-year Tribulation, before those terrible four horsemen ever ride onto the scene. The four horsemen, remember, are judgments from God. They are God's wrath being poured out on a Christ-rejecting world. The New Testament, however, assures us that God's church, the bride of Christ, is exempt from God's wrath.

Read what God says about this.

...and to wait for His Son from heaven, whom He raised from the dead, that is Jesus, who rescues us from the wrath to come. (1 Thessalonians 1:10)

For God has not destined us for wrath, but for obtaining salvation through our Lord Jesus Christ. (1 Thessalonians 5:9)

"Because you have kept the word of My perseverance, I also will keep you from the hour of testing, that hour which is about to come upon the whole world, to test those who dwell on the earth." (Revelation 3:10)

Also, did you ever notice that the church is not mentioned in Revelation 4–19, while the Tribulation period is being unleashed on the earth? The word *ekklesia* ("church") occurs twenty times in the book of Revelation. It occurs nineteen times in Revelation 1–3, and then not again until Revelation 22:16. And between these two points, the church is strangely absent from the biblical account of events on earth. To me this is strong evidence that the church will not be present on earth during the Tribulation.

To put it simply, Christ will come *for* His saints at the Rapture. And then, at least seven years later, He will come *with* His saints at the Second Coming.

The Rapture is our blessed hope.

CHAPTER EIGHT

READY TO RIDE?

In the movie *The Lord of the Rings: The Return of the King,* Gandalf the great wizard sees everything coming rapidly into place for the great battle—a battle for the very survival of Middle Earth. At one crucial juncture, he says, "The board is set, and the pieces are beginning to move."

Using this chess board metaphor, we could say the same thing about our world today. The board appears to be set. The pieces and players are in place. And the four horsemen, the riders who get it all started, could start moving at any point. All we're waiting for is the rapture of the church to heaven.

I believe that what we are witnessing in the world today points toward what the Bible predicts for the end times. Just look around, and you can see all kinds of signs that the four horsemen of the Apocalypse appear ready to ride.

Stop and consider. What are those forces, events, and circumstances we see converging before our eyes that make the world we live in today especially vulnerable to the scenes of devastation and destruction predicted in Revelation 6:1–8?

- Terrorism, the rise of militant Islam, and the desperate cry for world peace, especially in the Middle East, make the world ripe for the coming of Antichrist and his peace plan. *The rider on the white horse appears to be mounting up.*
- The invention and proliferation of modern weapons of mass destruction have paved the way for the bloodletting of warfare unlike anything this world has ever seen. *The red horse of war is moving into place.*
- Worldwide famine for the masses in the wake of modern weapons of mass destruction is guaranteed. And the exemption of the wealthy from this famine—in keeping with what we see as the divide between rich and poor in many parts of the world—is growing wider. *The black horse of famine is ready to follow.*
- Thirty new diseases have cropped up in just the

last thirty years. AIDS is decimating an entire continent. And globalism, with rapid means of travel, is the perfect vehicle to spread these plagues all over the earth with lightning speed. It's just a matter of time until the time bomb of pestilence explodes across our planet. *The pale horse is ready to sweep the globe, with Hades racing behind.*

John Walvoord observed world movements that signal the unleashing of the four horsemen.

There is much in the modern world which seems to portend just such a period. The introduction of modern means of warfare with new capacity to destroy life and property, the shrinking of the world by rapid transportation, and invention of modern weapons of war make all the earth vulnerable to such scenes of devastation and destruction of human life in the event of world conflict. The darkness of the human hour is in sharp contrast to the bright hope of the imminent return of Christ for His church as an event preceding the time of trouble.[40]

RAPTURE OR WRATH?

What all this means to you and me is very simple.

It's either Rapture or wrath.

If the Rapture comes within our lifetime, every person who reads these words will either be caught up to heaven to be with Christ (and return with Him at His Second Coming) or will experience the terror and desolation of the four horsemen. You will either ride a white horse with Christ when He returns or be trampled by those dreadful riders who gallop across the horizon, with hell and tribulation in their wake.

Rapture or wrath? That's the decision we all face.

So how can you and I be sure that we will be ready when the Rapture comes? How can we have full assurance that we have eternal life? The Bible says very plainly that God gives salvation from sin's penalty and forgiveness to all who will simply call upon His name. The Bible says you receive God's free gift of salvation provided by Christ's death on the cross by simply calling on the Lord in prayer. Romans 10:13 says, "WHOEVER WILL CALL ON THE NAME OF THE LORD WILL BE SAVED." All you have to do is call out to the Lord in true faith and say, "Lord, save me!"

It's the greatest decision you will ever make. When you receive Christ personally as your Savior from sin, you will immediately receive forgiveness for all your sins. For the very first time in your life, you will enter into a relationship with the living God.

Why not call upon the Lord right now to receive His gracious pardon by praying a simple prayer like the one below? There are no magic words that will bring salvation. God looks at the heart.

But if this prayer expresses the sincere desire of your heart to receive Christ as your personal Savior, God will save you right now. However and wherever you may be.

Father, I come to You now and admit that I'm a sinner. And I know that I need a Savior. I acknowledge that I can never earn my own way to heaven. I accept Jesus as the Savior I need. I believe that He died on the cross and rose again for me. I call upon You to save me. Thank You for saving me and allowing me to know You personally. Amen.

COME

In his massive study on Revelation, W. A. Criswell ends his section on the four horsemen with these stirring words of invitation:

> O Lord, may it be that we shall bow only before the one true God, that we may give our lives to the one true Prince, that we shall be numbered among those who call upon His name.... It is always dark for the wicked... always dark for Satan...always dark when sin reigns in the earth. But it is always light for the people of God. In the days of the flood there was an ark for the family of the people of God. In the days of the Israelites there were cities of refuge for the one who had inadvertently shed innocent blood, who fell into sin, who asked God's forgiveness.
>
> ...There is a refuge today for God's people. Though I face death tomorrow, yet, if I face Him today, my home, my refuge is not in the grave. The glory of God is not under the ground. The glory of God is in the pavilions of the heavens. God's people have their house

and their home and their destiny above the skies. For God's people there is glory and light and victory and heaven. That is the call the Lord extends in this day of grace to your heart. Come. Come. Come with us. In our march to glory, march with us. In a prayer of adoration, pray with us. In a hymn of love, sing with us.... Do it, and God will speed you and bless you as you come.[41]

If you have never personally come to Christ for salvation from sin, may you come now and receive cleansing.

If you have come to Christ in genuine faith, may you go forth armed with the power of His Spirit to live for Him, until He comes to catch us away to the Father's house.

1. Billy Graham, *Approaching Hoofbeats: The Four Horsemen of the Apocalypse* (Waco, TX: Word Books, 1983), 9, 12.
2. Ibid., 10.
3. Robert L. Thomas, *Revelation 1–7: An Exegetical Commentary* (Chicago: Moody Press, 1992), 380.
4. Ibid.
5. Graham, *Approaching Hoofbeats*, 10.
6. It's important to understand that taking things in the Bible as symbols does not in any way contradict the idea of literal interpretation of the Bible. Literal interpretation means that we try to discover the one meaning of the text that was originally intended by the author by taking into account the context, grammar, and historical background of a particular passage. Literal interpretation encompasses both what we call "plain-literal" and "figurative-literal" language.
7. This view is held by several excellent commentators, including James Montgomery Boice, *God's Word Today,* May 2002 (Philadephia, PA), 32–33; Leon Morris, *Revelation,* rev. ed., Tyndale New Testament Commentaries, (Grand Rapids, MI: Wm. B. Eerdmans, 1989), 100–101.
8. George Eldon Ladd, *A Commentary on the Revelation* (Grand Rapids, MI: Wm. B. Eerdmans, 1972), 99.
9. Ibid.
10. Ibid.
11. Donald Grey Barnhouse, *Revelation: An Expository Commentary* (Grand Rapids, MI: Zondervan, 1971), 122.
12. Thomas, *Revelation 1–7*, 421; W. A. Criswell, *Expository Sermons on Revelation, Five Volumes Complete and*

Unabridged in One, vol. 3 (Grand Rapids, MI: Zondervan, 1969), 92.

13. Daniel K. K. Wong, "The First Horseman of Revelation 6," *Bibliotheca Sacra* 153 (April–June 1996): 224.

14. Graham, *Approaching Hoofbeats,* 78.

15. David Jeremiah, *Escape the Coming Night* (Dallas, TX: Word Publishing, 1997), 112.

16. Charles H. Dyer, *World News and Bible Prophecy* (Wheaton, IL: Tyndale House Publishers, 1995), 214.

17. H. L. Willmington, *The King Is Coming* (Wheaton, IL: Tyndale House Publishers, 1973), 95.

18. Morris, *Revelation,* 113.

19. Jeremiah, *Escape the Coming Night,* 113.

20. Roy B. Zuck, *The Speaker's Quote Book* (Grand Rapids, MI: Kregel Publications, 1997), 407.

21. Thomas, *Revelation 1–7,* 429.

22. Graham, *Approaching Hoofbeats,* 128.

23. Ibid., 161.

24. Thomas, *Revelation 1–7,* 430.

25. John F. Walvoord, *The Revelation of Jesus Christ* (Chicago: Moody Press, 1966), 129.

26. Morris, *Revelation,* 116; Thomas, *Revelation 1–7,* 432–34.

27. In A.D. 92, in the face of a grain shortage, the Roman emperor Domitian ordered half of the vineyards of Asia Minor destroyed to make room for growing more grain. This resulted in riots in Asia Minor because wine was a major source of income in that area. In response, Domitian revoked his earlier edict and ordered that anyone who allowed their vineyards to go out of production would be prosecuted. This was a familiar picture for John's readers of

a case when grain was in shortage, but when it was illegal to harm the supply of oil and wine. Some believe that this prophecy in Revelation 6:5–6 was fulfilled in this edict of Domitian. However, I believe this will be fulfilled in the end times during the first half of the seven-year Tribulation. Domitian's edict served as an excellent contemporary illustration of Revelation 6:5–6, but not a fulfillment of it.

28. Thomas, *Revelation 1–7,* 436.
29. Ibid., 437.
30. The word Jesus used for *plagues* in Luke 21:11 is the Greek word *loimoi.* While it's different from the word John uses in Revelation 6:7 *(thanato),* both words describe sweeping plagues of the end times. Thomas, *Revelation 1–7,* 435.
31. Ibid., 439.
32. Henry Morris, *The Revelation Record* (Wheaton, IL: Tyndale House Publishers, 1983), 117–18.
33. John Phillips, *Exploring Revelation* (Neptune, NJ: Loizeaux Brothers, 1991), 105.
34. Adrian Rogers, *Unveiling the End Times in Our Time* (Nashville, TN: Broadman & Holman, 2004), 89–90.
35. Geoffrey Crawley, "How Progress Makes Us Sick," *Newsweek* (5 May 2003), 34.
36. Ibid.
37. Morris, *Revelation,* 393.
38. Ibid.
39. Robert L. Thomas, *Revelation 8–22* (Chicago: Moody Press, 1995), 387.
40. Walvoord, *The Revelation of Jesus Christ,* 133.
41. W. A. Criswell, *Expository Sermons on Revelation,* 100.

THE TRUTH BEHIND FICTION

The Left Behind books raise powerful and disturbing questions? *Do the authors present an accurate view of end time events? Could we really be that close to those final, terrible years? Do believers dare hope for a rapture that will sweep us into the presence of Christ before God unleashes His righteous judgment on the world?* If these things are true, it will certainly change the way we live our lives right now—giving us both a sense of urgency and an enduring hope.

www.endtimeanswers.com